Gold on Ice

Gold on Ice

The Salé and Pelletier Story

BEVERLEY SMITH

KEY PORTER BOOKS

Picture Credits

The Globe and Mail:
Fred Lum p 2, 55, 80

Brian Dole: p 32, 34

Marc Evon: p 6, 10, 12, 14, 15, 16, 19, 21, 22, 26, 29, 32

Stephan Potopnyk: p 8, 9, 18, 25, 36

Canapress Photo Archives:
Chuck Stoody, p 28, 33
Paul Chiasson p 38, 40, 43, 45, 47, 50, 70, 72
Frank Gunn p 54, 68
Ian Barrett p 57
Tony Bock (Toronto Star) p 59
Adrian Wyld p 77

Wide World Archive (AP):
Katsumi Kasahara p 30
Jacques Brinon p 35
Amy Sancetta p 41
Lionel Cironneau p 44, 46, 60, 62, 63, 64, 74
Doug Mills p 49
Robert Borea p 56
Georges Bakajlo p 58
Laurent Rebours p 61

Canadian Olympic Association:
André Forget p 42, 51, 73, 75, 78
Mike Ridewood p 52

National Library of Canada Cataloguing in Publication Data

Smith, Beverley, 1954–
    Gold on ice : the Salé and Pelletier story / Beverley Smith.

ISBN 1-55263-466-3

    1. Sale, Jamie, 1977–. 2. Pelletier, David, 1974–
3. Skaters—Canada—Biography. I. Title.

GV850.A2S55 2002   796.91'092'271   C2002-901487-5

The publisher gratefully acknowledges the support of the Canada Council for the Arts and the Ontario Arts Council for its publishing program.

We acknowledge the financial support of the Government of Canada through the Book Publishing Industry Development Program (BPIDP) for our publishing activities.

Key Porter Books Limited
70 The Esplanade
Toronto, Ontario
Canada M5E 1R2

www.keyporter.com

Design: Peter Maher
Electronic formatting: Jean Lightfoot Peters

Printed and bound in Canada

02 03 04 05 06 5 4 3 2 1

Contents

Introduction

I t takes a long time to become a figure skater, and a long time to become an Olympic judge. Neither job is easy at the best of times. There isn't a lot of money in it for most. Judges are volunteers, who get their expenses paid to do their work. Only the top handful of figure skaters make millions. Most toil without recognition in the trenches of cold arenas.

A skating judge is subject to all kinds of pressures and in the Olympic arena, the pressures are ratcheted upward with an incredible force. Issues that nobody cares about in the ordinary light of day gain brilliant importance in the glaring Olympic spotlight. After all, the Olympics happen only every four years, and if you win, the rewards are bountiful. What you do and how you behave at the Olympic Games should matter, big time. But it's an inescapable fact that Olympic rewards and bragging rights matter, too, sometimes for all the wrong reasons. At the Salt Lake City Olympics, the skating federations forgot about the athletes, who are expected to snuffle it up for the good of the country. The unwritten rule was that silence was golden. Be quiet and wait your turn, they were told.

During the 1940s and 1950s, Austrian federations played the games, swapping votes and making deals, trying to hold onto a diminishing power. When the Soviets caught wind that the Olympic Games meant something, they jumped in and in a short time, figured out how to work the crowd, a bit of caviar here, a few bottles of vodka there, doing what one dance coach called "buttering you up." In a short time, the Soviets became an incredible skating power and others began to play the games with them. After all, it takes two to tango. Over decades, a culture of dickering and dealing became entrenched. If you fought it, you suffered later. In this climate, you couldn't afford to annoy anybody.

But just before the Nagano Olympics, a few judges began to break ranks, understanding how wrong the system was, and how it could ultimately threaten the lifeblood of the burgeoning sport. They began to talk, but were quickly silenced by their federations, noting the International Skating Union rules that forbade judges to criticize officials and other judges. Even skaters were forbidden from speaking out by international federation rules. Just at a time when some

Salé and Pelletier skate with grace and style in their formative years together.

8

Salé (opposite page) and
Pelletier at Skate Canada 2000.

were calling for more open procedures, International Skating Union
president Ottavio Cinquanta announced at a press conference that
he saw no reason at all why judges had to explain their marks at all
to anyone. The problems weren't solved. They seethed. At the Salt
Lake City Olympics, they boiled over in unexpected places. And
Jamie Salé and David Pelletier were as shocked as anybody when
the ugliness spilled over into their event, the pairs discipline.

The Early Days

I t doesn't matter where you come from; the human spirit flourishes everywhere. It can be nourished in Red Deer, Alberta, population 50,000, and it can grow in Sayabec, Quebec, population 2,000. And it has. Who would have guessed that two young Canadians with big ideas would find themselves at the centre of the biggest judging scandal of the Salt Lake City Olympic Games, a controversy that raged for days, diverted attention from other sports, and turned Jamie Salé and David Pelletier into international celebrities overnight?

Salé and Pelletier didn't seek all the attention, which culminated in a stampede of cameras and big boots that swept bodies under foot, when they were leaving a press conference in Salt Lake City. Salé found herself frightened for her safety, yet, through it all, the fetching couple conducted themselves with dignity and class, blamed no one, and charmed everyone with their humour, including TV hosts Jay Leno and Larry King. In the span of a few days, they jumped from being a pair loved in the close figure skating world to household names. And this was all before the International Olympic Committee decided to turn their silver medals into gold. Their lives will never be the same.

Salé was a tiny thing, with a bright smile and big coffee bean eyes, when her parents Patti and Gene Salé unleashed her onto a figure skating rink at age five in Red Deer. She was a natural, and loved the spotlight. Salé used to tug on the coattails of her coach Debbie Wilson, and say: "Watch me! Watch me!" By the time she was eight, she had decided she was Olympic material.

She started out as a singles skater, and was impressed when Kurt Browning, who later won four world titles, stopped by Red Deer to do some ice shows. "He was doing big jumps, and he was cute," Salé said. "Everyone was fussing over him. You knew that he was a big-city skater. It all started with him."

Salé was only 10 when the Olympic Games came to nearby Calgary in 1988. It was the first time Salé remembers watching a major skating competition. At school, they discussed the Games. She remembers watching Elizabeth Manley winning an Olympic silver medal and wanted to be just like her. "I don't even remember

watching her program, but it was that walk she does at the end, and her running on the ice with the cowboy hat on," she said. Christine Hough was her next heroine. Hough was a pair skater who won the Canadian title with partner Doug Ladret in 1989. Like Salé, Hough was a performer who could light up a rink with her eyes. "When I first came into skating, she was really the only one in seniors who would talk to me," Salé said. "This girl was so cute and bubbly."

It was a different story for David Pelletier in Sayabec, a little town near the Gaspé Peninsula in Quebec; he was a little more reluctant. His mother, Murielle, signed him up for lessons when he was only three years old. His father, Jacques, thought it would help improve his hockey skills. But Pelletier didn't want to have anything to do with figure skating. "I didn't really like it," he said. His mother pushed him out the door onto the street on Tuesday nights, "getting my butt out to the rink," he said. "I had to do figures and dance, and I hated it. The only thing I liked doing was jumping. She did run after me to get me to the rink." There was no artificial ice in little Sayabec at the time, so Pelletier began his skating career on a rooftop with an ice surface, and waddled disinterestedly through all of his tests. He quit compulsory figures a couple of times, sneaking off to play street hockey instead, until a coach told him he had to do figures, because it was part of competitions.

Street hockey was more Pelletier's style. He was an active kid who played soccer, took up swimming, and played in a peewee minor hockey league. "We had to pull him out of the street to go to skating," said Murielle, a high school teacher. "It was not easy." Pelletier didn't even look much like a figure skater. "At the time, the one-piece suit was in style," Murielle said. "And he was a bit chubby." Although his two brothers, Martin and Mathieu, also took figure skating lessons, Pelletier quickly became Public Enemy No. 1. At the club, he'd make trouble, refuse to listen, pester the girls. The club president told his mother he didn't have any talent.

Everything changed when Pelletier watched the Calgary Olympics on television. The Olympics, he said, creates heroes once every four years, and it did that for him. He'd never heard of Brian Orser before the 1988 Olympics, a time when the eight-time Canadian champion and two-time Olympic silver medalist was ending his amateur career. But after Pelletier watched Isabelle Brasseur and Lloyd Eisler finish ninth at the Olympic Games in Calgary, he became a pair skater, too, teaming up with Julie Laporte.

To reach this new goal, Pelletier had to leave home at age 13 and board in Rimouski to train with coach David Graham, who had started a pair skating school there. At first, Pelletier was enthusiastic

There was no artificial ice in Sayabec, Quebec, so Pelletier began his skating career on a rooftop with an ice surface. He quit compulsory figures a couple of times, sneaking off to play street hockey instead, until a coach told him he had to do figures, because it was part of competitions.

14

Pelletier became enamored
of skating after watching the
Calgary Olympics on television.
The Olympics, he said, creates
heroes once every four years,
and it did that for him.

about leaving to live in the town of 60,000, 30 times the size of the village he'd come from. But when he arrived, he found it hard. He knew no one. When he phoned home crying, his parents wondered if they had done the right thing in letting him go. He'd call sometimes and tell them, "I quit. I've had enough." Then they wouldn't hear from him for a few days, and he'd be back at work, training, and going to school.

"It was not fun," Pelletier said. "It was a huge change." He arrived at his boarding home in Rimouski the night before school started and remembered with dismay the teacher asking students to give their address and phone number in front of the class. "I'm standing there alone, before the bell rings," he said. "It's a brand new school. Nobody had set foot in it. I sit down, and we go through the address and phone numbers for everybody. Then it gets to me. I'm in Grade Eight, and I don't know my address and phone number. It was an awful experience."

Pelletier also had to explain to his class that he was a figure skater, at an age where he'd be razzed for taking part in a "girl's sport. He had to rush off to the principal's office and look up the phone number in a phone book. "It was very embarrassing," he said. "Not a good first step to make friends." 'Hey, look at the loser. He's a figure skater. Doesn't even know his phone number.'"

But Pelletier wasn't a loser at all, and nobody knew that they had just met a future Olympic champion.

Pelletier left home at age 13 for Rimouski, Quebec to train with coach David Graham, who had started a pair skating school there—a town of 60,000, 30 times the size of the village Pelletier had come from.

Two Solitudes

There was always a brightness and a promise about the careers in both Jamie Salé and David Pelletier, even when they were moving up through the ranks in Canada at opposite ends of the country. Both leaped from success to success. They were noticed right from the beginning. Two years after the Calgary Olympics, Salé finished third at the Canadian championships in Sudbury in novice pairs with her partner Jason Turner. Strangely enough, they finished behind Shae-Lynn Bourne, who skated pairs before she turned to ice dancing and became a four-time world bronze medalist with Victor Kraatz. Salé had just moved to Edmonton to train with Swedish-born coach Jan Ullmark, known as one of the country's great technical coaches and a father-like figure, very cultured and well educated. Salé was a handful, full of life and fire, and in response, Ullmark threw her off the ice one day.

At the time, Pelletier was still in Rimouski, trying to find his feet. "For the first year I was there, I didn't do anything," Pelletier said. "It was just a period when I had to adjust. The second year, I was fine. I stopped missing my parents so much and my friends. I had a life somewhere else. It took a long time." His hero was Francois Beaulieu, a Rimouski skater who qualified for the 1989 Canadian championships and finished 16th among 16 in the junior men's event. To Pelletier, this was a big deal.

By 1991, Pelletier finally qualified for the Canadian championships himself, in Saskatoon, Saskatchewan. Teamed with Julie Laporte, Pelletier won a bronze medal in novice pairs. But by then, Salé was already a little star from the west. She had stepped up to the junior level and, at their first crack at it, she and Turner won the silver medal, even earning a few first-place marks from judges for their long program.

The Canadian Figure Skating Association had already started to give the two young skaters its blessing. Salé and Turner began getting international assignments, finishing third at a competition in Obertsdorf, Germany. The Canadian Figure Skating Association saw such promise in Laporte and Pelletier that it sent them to the junior

Pelletier finally qualified for the Canadian championships himself by 1991, in Saskatoon, Saskatchewan. Teamed with Julie Laporte, Pelletier won a bronze medal in novice pairs. But by then, Salé had stepped up to the junior level and, at their first crack at it, she and Turner won the silver medal, even earning a few first-place marks from judges for their long program.

Far Right: **The Canadian Figure Skating Association gave the two young skaters its blessing. Salé and Turner began getting international assignments.**

Salé began keeping an eye on Pelletier as a potential partner—on her own accord and at the encouragement of others.

world championships in Hull, Quebec, where they finished very respectably in fifth.

Although Pelletier was three years older than Salé, he was still on the novice track in 1992. He looked up to Salé, who won the junior pairs title with Turner at the Canadian championships in Moncton, New Brunswick. Pelletier walked away with a gold medal too—but at the lower level, in novice pairs with Laporte. He also was good enough to qualify for the junior men's singles event, but finished at the bottom of the pack.

Nevertheless, something important happened that year that changed the course of Pelletier's life. He attended a sports gala in Rimouski that honoured 1992 Olympic silver medalist Guillaume Leblanc, a racewalker from Rimouski. Pelletier got a chance to look at and touch Leblanc's medal. It was stark evidence that someone from a small town in Quebec could reach the top. Pelletier told his parents: "One day, I'm going to get one of those. I don't know what colour, but I'm going to get one."

After the sports gala, Pelletier's focus intensified. He had already taken on extra work, skating both singles and pairs, and was slim and fit, with strong shoulders. By the 1993 Canadian championships, his efforts started to pay off. He finished second behind Ravi Walia in the junior men's event, and easily won the junior pairs title with Laporte, getting first-place marks from every judge.

In Edmonton, thousands of miles away, Salé, too, was working hard. Skating with Turner, she finished fourth behind eventual world champions Isabelle Brasseur and Lloyd Eisler in the senior pairs event at the 1993 Canadian championships. And as a singles skater, she finished eighth in the junior women's event, ahead of Jennifer Robinson, who went on to become a five-time Canadian champion.

The 1994 and 1995 seasons were watershed years for Salé and Pelletier. Both would experience the highs of the sport and humbling defeats. Pelletier later called them "humility lessons." Salé and Turner earned a trip to the Lillehammer Olympics by finishing third at the 1994 Canadian championships in Edmonton. In Lillehammer, they finished 12th, and after a 16th place finish at the world championships in Japan, their partnership dissolved. So did Salé's pairs career, at least for the next three years.

During the 1994 season, Pelletier began a four-year partnership with Allison Gaylor, and learned that sometimes you take baby steps with a new partner until you bond. They finished eighth at the Canadian championships at the senior level. Both Salé and Pelletier won bronze medals in junior singles events.

By the following season, Gaylor and Pelletier were rolling. They

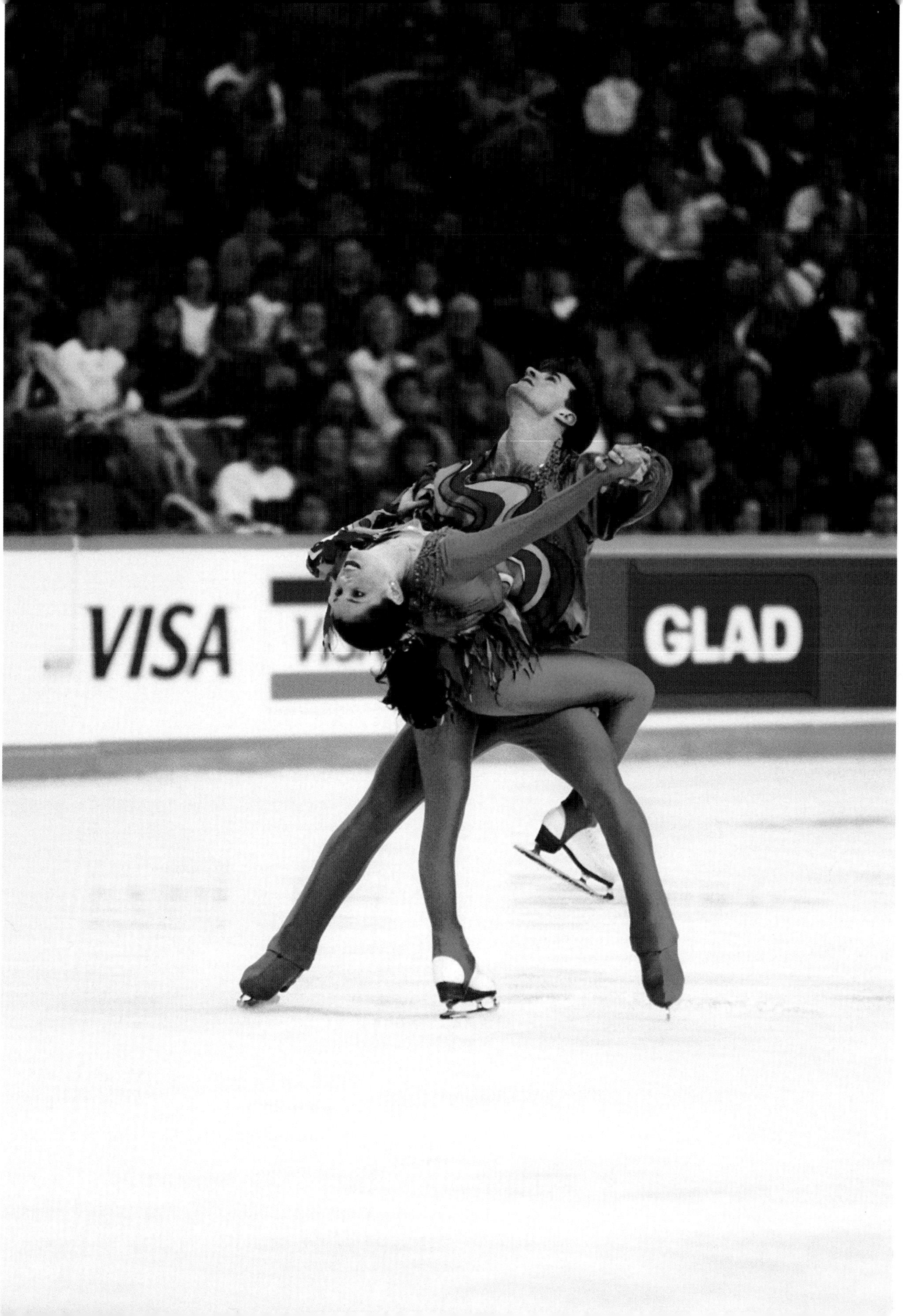
VISA
GLAD

20

In 1996, both Pelletier and Salé's careers took a downturn. Salé didn't make it to the Canadian Championships in 1996 and 1997, and Pelletier's partner developed knee problems.

finished second at the 1995 Canadian championships in Halifax and, with Pelletier's gregarious personality shining through, earned a standing ovation. Pelletier thrust his fist into the air and picked Gaylor up off the ice. The large crowd fell in love with them, and booed their marks.

Pelletier also finished fourth in the senior men's event, after being second in the short program, and the national media began to show an interest. He and Gaylor made it to the world championships in Birmingham, finishing 15th. As his career was soaring, Salé was going it alone, finishing fifth in the senior women's singles, and looking wistfully for a partner. Her singles effort was impressive enough for the Canadian Figure Skating Association to send her to the junior world championships, where she finished 12th.

Pelletier saw Salé's sparkle, and he quietly began to watch her, admitting he was intimidated by the cocky little star from the west. She had noticed him, too, especially after a summer training camp. In the fall of 1995, coach Cynthia Ullmark returned home from the Nations Cup international competition in Germany, after seeing Pelletier compete, and told Salé: "You know, there's a really great partner out there for you. His name is David Pelletier." There was one big problem: Pelletier already had a partner. Even so, the following year, Pelletier had a tryout with Salé. It didn't work out; they didn't click. Pelletier continued to skate with Gaylor, and Salé continued on her own. Pelletier had moved to Montreal to train with Josée Picard, Brasseur and Eisler's coach and, to make extra money, was serving beer and hot dogs at the Montreal Forum for $10 an hour. Salé was working as a waitress in a coffee shop in Edmonton.

But Salé didn't forget Pelletier. Every chance she got, she kept her eye on him. "It was hard," she said. "He was from the east and I was from the west. I was young, too. I wasn't ready to move to Quebec at all. I was a little bit afraid to leave what I had in Edmonton. He wasn't ready to move to Alberta, either. It was kind of a blessing that it didn't work out."

In 1996, both of their careers took a downtown. Salé failed to make it to the Canadian championships in 1996 and 1997. Pelletier's results weren't fulfilling the promise he had shown in 1995. He finished fifth with Gaylor at the 1996 Canadian championships. Then, Gaylor began to develop knee problems and required surgery. The pair finished last at one competition. "For the first time in my life, I was finishing last," Pelletier said. "Looking back, it really wasn't that bad. But at the time, I felt I was not doing anything with my life."

He spent one more year with Gaylor, and finished sixth at the

1997 Canadian championships. Then things began to unravel. He couldn't handle the fall from second to fifth or sixth, and began to develop a bad attitude. He realized later he hadn't been very supportive or patient with Gaylor, who quit.

Pelletier skated pairs one year with Caroline Roy, but when they finished only sixth at the 1998 Canadian championships, Pelletier was discouraged. "I was almost ready to hang up my skates," he said. "I was tired of sixth-place finishes and 15th-place finishes at worlds."

Sixth-place finishes at Canadian championships weren't good enough to make world teams, or national teams. Without a spot on the national team, Pelletier lost a chance to get international assignments and much-needed financing. The future looked bleak.

In Edmonton, Salé was facing hard facts. She was stunned one day when her mother Patti and her stepfather told her she had to buckle down to work at skating, or they wouldn't pay the bills anymore. People had actually figured she'd quit. "I wasn't sure where I was really going sometimes," she said. "I didn't really have a clear head. I knew what I wanted, but it wasn't meant to be. I needed that three years to be by myself and experience things for myself. I learned a lot and I think I'm a better person for it."

Ironically, both Salé and Pelletier made last-ditch efforts to salvage their careers. Early in 1998, Pelletier approached Montreal coach Richard Gauthier. Gauthier had heard nasty rumours about Pelletier's temper and wasn't sure he wanted an unsettling influence in his club. "He heard that I treated my partners really bad, I was an extreme perfectionist, and that I used to kick the ice and yell at my partner," Pelletier said."Before I even had a lesson with him, he based his opinion of me on reputation, and I think that was a little unfair."

Pelletier promised Gauthier he'd do anything he asked, and Gauthier reluctantly took him on, but only after setting some ground rules. Pelletier was eager to listen. Gauthier was the kind of teacher who brooked no nonsense on the ice, who was intent on making his students good people as well as skaters. Pelletier couldn't have fallen into better hands. Gauthier told him there was only one partner for him: Jamie Salé. They arranged a four-day tryout with Salé in Edmonton.

Salé's tryout with Pelletier was magical. "It was everything I hoped for and more," Salé said later. "You don't really believe it until it happens. When we tried out, we kind of blew each other away." They tried a triple twist. It just happened. Throw jumps just happened, too. There were obviously some timing differences they

During the 1994 season, Pelletier began a four-year partnership with Allison Gaylor, and learned that sometimes you take baby steps with a new partner until you bond. They finished eighth at the Canadian championships at the senior level.

Salé and Turner skate at the
1993 Canadian Championships.

had to work out, but everything seemed easy. "The first time we did side-by-side spins, they matched," Salé said. "It was unbelievable. That was something I had a hard time with, with my other partner. We had to work on it a long time."

As soon as Pelletier returned to Montreal, his phone rang. It was Salé. They decided to make the partnership work. To do this, Salé had to leave Edmonton for Montreal. She spoke no French, and rushed headlong into culture shock. The training atmosphere was different in Montreal as well. While the West had a more laid-back ambience, Salé found more edginess training in Montreal. Skaters were competitive with each other. Perhaps, she thought, that's why so many Quebec skaters excelled on the international stage. But at age 20, Salé was ready to become independent and live her own life. "I was exactly where I wanted to be." she said.

In Salé and Pelletier, Gauthier was presented with an interesting problem: the combination of personalities. Pelletier had skated with partners who either looked up to him or didn't quarrel with his attitude. Salé didn't take any nonsense. "I thought: 'How am I going to get these two brains to work together?'" Gauthier said. One approach was to ask Salé and Pelletier to work through a set of 30 Anthony Robbins motivational tapes. Pelletier learned that he had to allow himself to make mistakes. "Failure is your best friend," Pelletier learned to tell himself. Because of Gauthier, Salé and Pelletier learned how to communicate, which has become their greatest asset on the ice.

In the following weeks, Salé and Pelletier became yin and yang, perfect halves of each other. Pelletier was a perfectionist; Salé was a performer, more concerned about where the music took her. Pelletier was a private person, more reserved, although he's known for his sense of humour and witty one-liners; Salé was bubbly and outgoing, with a smile that could melt hearts. For the first time, they understood what it meant to trust a partner, to reach out a hand and know the other was there, to know and believe the other would fight for that perfect performance. It was the last shot for both at finding the golden ring in figure skating. Everybody who understood figure skating in Canada knew this partnership could be magic—it was meant to be.

Together at Last

Jamie Salé and David Pelletier have a curious history of being on the brink of brilliance when they suffer a lurching setback. Their career together has always followed a winding path, strewn with roadblocks and detours. Finally together, they should have soared into the skating stratosphere straight away. But it wasn't to be.

Their new partnership was born on March 10, 1998, but they jumped into things so quickly that Salé ended up with tendonitis. They missed 2 ½ months of training after she underwent surgery to repair her Achilles tendon, a serious injury. With only five months to figure out programs, straighten out their timing and unison, and get physically fit, they caught a break: the Canadian Figure Skating Association invited them to Skate Canada, a major international event, even though they were unranked skaters at home and therefore not members of the national team.

Amazingly enough, even though they had been playing catch-up after the injury, and Salé hadn't skated pairs in four years, she and Pelletier stunned everybody at Skate Canada in Kamloops, B.C., winning a bronze medal and defeating two Canadian pair champions. Salé and Pelletier were second in the short program, behind world medalists Shen Xue and Zhao Hongbo of China. They even won one first-place mark from a Russian judge, who placed them ahead of new Russian pair Maria Petrova and Alexei Tikhonov.

"We don't know what to expect from the marks," Pelletier said at the time. "We don't even know where we rank in Canada. I told Jamie at the beginning not to expect anything." Because they were a new team, they didn't get the level of financial support from the skating association that others did, and they didn't qualify for the monthly cheques the federal government sends athletes. Nevertheless, so promising was their effort that the CFSA managed to get them invited to the NHK Trophy in Japan, too. The $US10,000 they earned from Skate Canada helped them pay to take Gauthier to Japan. "Now I can pay for it before 1999," Pelletier quipped. In Japan, they earned a bronze medal, and just missed qualifying for the Grand Prix Final.

Then tragedy struck during the 1998-99 season. They finished

Salé and Pelletier's new partnership was born on March 10, 1998, but they jumped into things so quickly that Salé ended up with tendonitis—the beginning of a series of setbacks that plagued the pair's early career together.

Above: **Pelletier guides Salé across the ice during pairs free skating competition at Skate Canada in 1998. The pair placed third in the competition.**

Far Right: **The first major break for the pair came when the Canadian Figure Skating Association invited them to Skate Canada, a major international event, even though they were unranked skaters at home and therefore not members of the national team. Events previous to the 2002 Olympics proved they were a major force in figure skating.**

second at the Canadian championships in their first try, behind Kristy Sargeant and Kris Wirtz, but didn't perform their "Night Train" or "Spirits of the People" routines again. Before the Canadian championships, Pelletier was already feeling the effects of a herniated disc. He limped his way through the event, but afterward, found himself unable to get out of bed. "I hurt my back at Christmas time and it just got worse and worse and worse," Pelletier said. The injury forced them to withdraw not only from the Four Continents Championships in Halifax but also the world championships in Helsinki.

Pelletier was forced to take 2 ½ months off training, and he carefully did whatever the doctor told him. "My lower back injury is from a lack of training," he said, with a twinkle. "Instead of doing my chest, I should have been working on my back. Chest is good on the beach." He may have been joking about it, but the problem frightened Salé and Pelletier, because it could have spelled the end of their careers.

Then, just before the 2001 world championships in Vancouver, destiny toyed with them again. Just before the event, a wall in their Montreal condominium caught on fire, ignited by a spark from a welding shop below. Then someone stole Pelletier's car. Salé spilled some burning coffee on her hand, which affected their training. Still, they won.

Salé and Pelletier's greatest nemeses have always been Russians Elena Berezhnaia and Anton Sikharulidze, who were already an established team when Salé and Pelletier joined forces. Known for their beautiful line, speed, and perfect unison, Berezhnaia and Sikharulidze were already two-time world champions and Olympic silver medalists when the two teams met for the first time at the 1998 NHK Trophy, only the second international competition of Salé and Pelletier's career. Berezhnaia and Sikharulidze won easily, getting first-place marks from all judges. Salé and Pelletier fought the Chinese team of Shen Xue and Zhao Hongbo to place third.

Salé and Pelletier would meet the Russians nine times leading up to the Olympic Games in Salt Lake City, and win six of those meetings. In spite of their relative lack of experience, the Canadians quickly put themselves on equal footing with the Russians in only their second season as a team. Salé and Pelletier came armed with the best tools in the trade: they had improved their technical tricks, and they had Canadian choreographer Lori Nichol to design their programs. Nichol dreamed up "Love Story," which silenced crowds during the 1999–2000 season.

Because they were a new team, Salé and Pelletier didn't get the level of financial support from the skating association that others did, and they didn't qualify for the monthly cheques the federal government sends athletes. The money they earned from Skate Canada helped them pay to take their coach to Japan.

Far Left: Pelletier lifts up Salé during the 1998 NHK Trophy figure skating competition pairs event in Saporo, Japan in December, 1998. They finished third.

And during this season, life copied art. Salé and Pelletier quietly began to develop their own real-life Love Story, despite the fact that Pelletier had already been married to a former pair skater. The two skaters grew close as they shared a new, exciting journey together. They became a couple, but talked little about it until Olympic season.

Salé and Pelletier first unleashed "Love Story" at the 1999 Skate America event in Colorado Springs, where they met six of the top-10-ranked teams in the world. It wasn't an easy way to start, but Gauthier was a brilliant strategist. He knew that the altitude of about 6,000 feet above sea level in Colorado Springs was staggering, about 2,000 feet higher than Salt Lake City. He sent Salé and Pelletier to Colorado Springs a week early to get used to it. His plan was to get them out of the starting blocks early, have them fit and ready for their very first event of the season, and then get people talking about them immediately. It worked. Salé and Pelletier became the buzz of the competition when they won both the short and long programs, and Berezhnaia and Sikharulidze faltered, finishing only fourth in the short program and third in the long, to garner a bronze medal. Everybody began to ask about this "unknown" Canadian team.

Berezhnaia and Sikharulidze had troubles the rest of the season, skating poorly at the Grand Prix Final in Lyon, finishing only third, with Salé and Pelletier fifth. Berezhnaia and Sikharulidze were forced to withdraw from the world championships in Nice when dope testing found a banned stimulant in Berezhnaia's urine. The door was wide open for Salé and Pelletier to win the world championships in their first try, but they made mistakes and finished fourth, in shock and in tears.

Since that setback, Salé and Pelletier have run up a long string of impressive victories through determination, never being content to rest on any kind of laurels, and always eager to improve. Their lifts have become supremely difficult, their throw jumps sound, with soft landings, their death spirals perfect, their twists easy. One of their hallmarks is that they make difficult things look easy. They radiate charm with their complex programs.

At the 2001 Canadian championships in Winnipeg, they earned five perfect marks of 6.0, and drew tears from former world pair champion Barbara Underhill. "In general, the Russians have always gone simpler, but with tons of quality and elegance," said coach Kim Hanford, of Toronto, who has given international seminars on pair skating. "In Canada, we tend to do tricker things and sometimes forgo the quality. But I think [Salé and Pelleter] are the first team to get away from that. They hold each position."

Salé and Pelletier performing in the pairs short program at Skate Canada in Kamloops. They became the surprise of the night, placing second in the competition ahead of the Canadian favorites Sargeant and Wirtz.

Far Left: At the 2001 Canadian championships in Winnipeg, they earned five perfect marks, and drew tears from former world pair champion Barbara Underhill.

In Vancouver in March 2001, the twosome made mistakes in the short program that were serious enough to drop them into third place, behind Berezhnaia and Sikharulidze, who were first. However, in the long program, Salé and Pelletier skated through a wall of noise and won first-place marks from six of the nine judges on the panel.

Far Right: Pelletier and Salé perform their pairs short program during the 14ᵗʰ Lalique Trophy figure skating event in Paris, November, 2000.

During the two seasons before the Olympic Games, Berezhnaia and Sikharulidze defeated Salé and Pelletier only once, at the Lalique Trophy in France during the 2000–01 season. However, for the preceding two seasons, the teams traded victories between short and long programs, and judging panels have always been closely divided on who to place first, with the Canadians often coming from behind to win.

Salé and Pelletier won their only world championship title this way, in Vancouver in March 2001. Feeling the pressure of skating to a large, noisy home crowd, the twosome made mistakes in the short program that were serious enough to drop them into third place, behind Berezhnaia and Sikharulidze, who were first. However, in the long program, Salé and Pelletier skated through a wall of noise and won first-place marks from six of the nine judges on the panel. The Russians, skating cleanly, got the rest.

At that event, Salé and Pelletier got a taste of what it would be like at the Olympic Games. Their world championship win was Canada's first world gold medal in pairs in eight years. The next morning, they awakened at 5:30 a.m. to do television interviews. Pelletier found, to his surprise, 25 messages on his answering machine. The attention was all new to them, but it get only more intense in the next year.

A moment of inspired confidence at Skate Canada 2000.

The Olympic Games

When Jamie Salé and David Pelletier set foot in Salt Lake City, they carried the burden of a nation on their shoulders. In only a few short years, they had become stars. After they won the world championships in Vancouver, they had left Gauthier, the coach who led them there, and went to Jan Ullmark. The move shocked everybody, and the skaters had to defend their decision as graciously as possible.

They no longer lived an invisible life, toiling in cold rinks; their faces were on Cheerios boxes. General Mills set up life-size cardboard cut-out photographs of them in food store aisles, leading Salé to joke that she had to avoid grocery stores. They couldn't train without adults and children watching their every stroke. They'd see, with some amusement, young figure skaters copying their moves. Bodyguards protected them on a few occasions at the Canadian championships in Hamilton, Ontario. In a country with a strong tradition of pair skating, they could make no mistakes. NBC, the host broadcaster for the Olympics, adopted them, using them extensively in advertisements to promote a North American battle against the 10-year supremacy of the Russians and Soviets in the Olympic pairs event.

And then, there was that other jinx to break. Although Canada had long been a figure skating power, the country hadn't won an Olympic figure skating gold medal in 42 years, since Barbara Wagner and Bob Paul won the pairs event in 1960. And the night that Salé and Pelletier skated their Olympic programs, Wagner and Paul were watching from front-row seats.

Salé and Pelletier had to deal with it, somehow. "We are not coming here to break a streak," Pelletier said. "There is not one human being I know that can take this on their shoulders." Thinking that Salt Lake City could be their only Olympics, Salé and Pelletier marched in the opening ceremonies, then had to defend this decision, too. They had to compete the next day, and shouldn't they rest? Four-time Olympian Lloyd Eisler, also a pair skater with early competitions, never missed the walk, they reasoned. Teammate Elvis Stojko urged them not to miss the opening ceremonies for anything;

Salé is thrown by Pelletier to win the silver medal in the pairs competition at the Olympic Winter Games in Salt Lake City. The crowd booed when it learned world champions Salé and Pelletier were placed second.

it was all part of the Olympic experience. They eagerly took his advice. Said Pelletier of the Olympic experience: "It's like two pounds of adrenaline up your butt."

When Salé and Pelletier faced the Olympic judges in the short program, they had won nine consecutive competitions. Elena Berezhnaia and Anton Sikharulidze had already run an exhausting gauntlet of injuries. During a practice lift last November, Berezhnaia slipped from Sikharulidze's grip, and her skate slashed his arm, almost forcing them out of the Grand Prix series. Then, they pulled out of the European championships only one month before the Olympics, with Berezhnaia suffering from a long-standing Achilles problem. Salé and Pelletier had muffed their long program at the Canadian championships, causing Pelletier to lose his cool, then sheepishly apologize to everybody afterward. All had inner battles to overcome.

In spite of it all, both teams skated performances worthy of Olympians. Salé and Pelletier skated their playful "Jalousie" tango routine with a sense of fun, landing every element with expertise, until the final pose, when both fell unexpectedly into a heap on the ice. The judges placed the Russians first and the Canadians second in a portion of the event worth one-third of the final mark. "We were

Far Left: **Salé and Pelletier perform their pairs free skate to win the Olympic silver medal at the XIX Olympic Winter Games in Salt Lake City, Utah.**

Salé and Pelletier enjoy a moment of hilarity after falling in the last seconds of their pairs short program during the Winter Olympics.

Far Left: Salé soars above
Pelletier during their Pairs Free
Skating in Salt Lake City, Utah,
initially winning a silver medal.

Salé is held by Pelletier during a
practice session in preparation
for the Olympic Winter Games.

Far Right: **Salé is helped up by Pelletier, left, and Russian skater Anton Sikharulidze after Salé and Sikharulidze collided during the warm up for the pairs free skate at the 2002 Olympic Winter Games.**

Gold medalists Salé and Pelletier perform during the 2002 Winter Olympic figure skating exhibition at the Salt Lake Ice Center.

Russian figure skaters Anton Sikharulidze and Elena Berezhnaia wait for their scores after competing in the pairs free program in the Winter Olympics at the Salt Lake Ice Center.

Far Right: Olympic gold medalist Anton Sikharulidze and his partner Elena Berezhnaia perform their free skate at the Winter Games.

Pelletier and Salé look up after completing their silver medal performace in the pairs competition at the Winter Olympics.

excited at the very end, and we were just trying to finish it strong…," Salé said. "I didn't even know I had fallen until I was on the ice. I'm backwards, upside down, all of a sudden. I'm laying there, and he's going: "I can't believe I came all the way to the Olympics to do this.' It was kind of cute." Only two judges of the nine—from Canada and Germany—ranked the Canadians first.

Salé and Pelletier seemed unworried. As long as they finished in the top three spots in the short program, they could still win the gold medal. Judges did not have to deduct marks from their miscue, because the fall didn't occur during a required element. Still, it gave judges an excuse to mark them down. Yet their fall was perhaps due to the luck of the draw. Six skaters had already competed before the Canadians took their opening pose, and there were many ruts on the ice. It was worse in the centre of the ice where many pairs had already done spins. Pelletier's blade hit one of the ruts just as he was about to swing Salé into the final tango pose, a move conjured up by four-time world champion Kurt Browning.. "Funniest thing for me, I'm supposed to have a surprised look on my face at the end," Salé said with a laugh. "I'm sure I did." They both were very aware that millions, perhaps billions of people were watching their every step.

There wasn't nearly as much to laugh about during the long program, for which Salé and Pelletier brought back their much-revered "Love Story" routine. To start off, Salé collided heavily with Sikharulidze during the six-minute warm-up. The accident pitched Salé to her knees, while Sikharulidze spun off onto his hands. As Salé knelt on the ice, stunned, Sikharulidze rushed over to help. It took the Canadian a long time to get up. "It really shook me up," Salé said afterward. "It knocked the wind out of me … When they came over to me, I couldn't move. I was almost paralyzed." Her head hurt. Her stomach hurt. Her arm went numb. She felt like she'd taken a hockey bodycheck. Then she looked up at Pelletier, her jaw set, and said: "I'm not finished. There's no way. I'm not giving up."

The Russians went out on the ice first, and skated beautifully to "Meditation" from the opera "Thais." Their most visible mistakes were Sikharulidze stepping out of a double Axel combination, and some rather unsteady throw jumps. Seven of the nine judges gave them marks of 5.9 out of 6.0 for presentation and a jumble of 5.7s and 5.8s for technique. Salé and Pelletier would have to be perfect to defeat them. And when it came time, the Canadians were perfect, in spite of all the pressure, the hype, and the hard collision. They skated as if on wings. They did not falter, not once. The crowd cheered wildly at every trick. The first hurrah erupted when both landed triple toe loops, an element that had troubled Salé in previous years.

Far Left: Salé hugs Pelletier at
the end their pairs free skate at
the 2002 Olympic Winter Games.

Pelletier holds Salé after hearing
their marks upon completing
their pairs free skating.

Seconds before the Canadians finished, a roar went up from the large crowd. At the completion of their program, Salé covered her face in her hands, and Pelletier knelt and kissed the ice. He pumped his fists into the air, joy in every muscle. After a long ovation, the crowd began to chant for perfect marks of 6.0. Past champion Barbara Wagner waved a little Canadian flag from her seat, and Bob Paul was on his feet, cheering.

The joy was shortlived. The first row of marks for technical merit came out: 5.7, 5.7, 5.8, 5.7, 5.7, 5.7, 5.7, 5.7, 5.7. Sitting in the kiss-and-cry area, Salé began to sob. She knew she had lost, without having seen the second set of marks for presentation. When it was clear that judges had collectively placed the Canadians second, the crowd began to jeer loudly. The reaction from others was swift. On NBC, commentator Sandra Bezic, a former Canadian pair skater and choreographer, said she felt embarrassed for her sport. Salé and Pelletier's choreographer, Lori Nichol, said she was ashamed of her sport, although she admitted having a bias toward her skaters. Ullmark couldn't believe his eyes. It didn't jibe with what had happened at the Grand Prix Final in Kitchener, Ontario, only two months before, when Salé and Pelletier had used their "Love Story" routine. The Russians had made one mistake, a big one; Berezhnaia had fallen on a throw jump, and the Canadians had skated perfectly. The seven judges had all ranked Salé and Pelletier first, with a couple of perfect marks of 6.0 to boot in that event. Remembering that, Ullmark couldn't explain to himself or to anybody else what had happened. "We've seen this in dance a lot," Ullmark said, speaking of the judging. "And now we're seeing it here, too. That's sad. The other events are a lot easier to judge and determine than dance. It wasn't fair."

While Salé was emotional, Pelletier maintained a stoic appearance during the difficult moments that followed the announcement of the marks. But later, his weary words of frustration boiled to the surface. "It was the worst six months of my life," he blurted out at a press conference. "So many sleepless nights. So many nightmares. The Olympic dream sometimes can turn into an Olympic nightmare." In his charming way (English is not his first language, and is not commonly spoken in Sayabec) he said: "I was shaking my pants before I got on (the ice)." He spoke of how tough it had been to skate without caving in to the pressure. In spite of all the emotions swirling around him, he felt relieved. "It's been six months," he said. "You go to the grocery store and it's, 'Bring back the gold.' You go to the hardware store: 'Bring back the gold.' I'm just there to buy a hammer, you know. It's everywhere. It's six months of people's expectations coming out of me."

Pelletier yells out after completing his pairs free skating with Jamie Salé in Salt Lake City, Utah Monday February 11, at the 2002 Winter Olympics.

Salé and Pelletier had expectations, too, of themselves. Quickly, and with grace, they put everything into perspective. When the marks came up, Pelletier admitted he was sad to be second. "I'm a human being," he said. The pair had no control of the marks. They had control only of what they did on the ice. "If I didn't want this to happen to me, I would have gone down the hill on skiis," he said. "We are so proud of what we did. I can't believe we did it like this. It was the toughest day of my life. And the longest."

The long day was about to turn into a long week. Over the next 48 hours, Salé and Pelletier got about two hours of sleep. What had happened to them awoke a protest that upstaged much of the Olympic Games. Salé and Pelletier may not have realized it at first, but they were at the centre of the biggest judging scandal to hit the Olympic Games.

Salé slides across the ice holding Pelletier's guiding hand.

Far Left: **Elena Berezhnaia and Anton Sikharulidze look eye to eye during their short program in the pairs competition.**

The Scandal Erupts

As soon as Jamie Salé and David Pelletier's marks went up, many things happened in Salt Lake City. When Canadian judge Benoit Lavoie saw that Salé and Pelletier had been placed second, he shook his head, and thumped his fist on the table. Several feet away sat German official Peter Krick, whose wife, Sissy, was on the pairs judging panel. She had voted for the Canadians to finish first. Krick had been hobbling around all week on crutches, and when the judges were about to leave their dais, he quickly sized up what had happened and took action. He stuck his crutch out in front of French judge Marie-Reine Le Gougne, and wouldn't let her pass until after the medal presentations, so she was forced to watch the tears trickle down Salé's cheeks.

Marie-Reine Le Gougne's name would come up again and again throughout the week. In fact, her name had already come up in the week before the Olympic Games started. "Watch out for the French judge in the pairs event," said a source from the ice dancing world, where vote-swapping and deal-making has been most rampant. The warning came before Salé and Pelletier had even landed in Salt Lake City to compete. Yet the judging panel in the pairs event didn't appear to be an event that would be affected by judging irregularities, with judges from Russia, China, United States, France, Poland, Canada, Ukraine, Germany, and Japan on it. If anything, it looked like a panel that should worry the Russians, who seemed to have few allies on it. It was completely unlike the dance panel. From the moment the 10 possible members of the ice dancing panel were drawn from a black bag with the names of 16 countries in it in Zagreb three months before the Olympics, it appeared stacked with countries whose judges seemed to have been voting in a bloc all season, including Russia, Ukraine, Israel, and Italy. One of the members of the ice dancing panel was Alla Shekhovtseva, wife of Valentin Piseev, president of the Russian skating federation. And the referee of the dance event—handpicked by International Skating Union president Ottavio Cinquanta, an Italian—was Alexander Gorshkov, a Russian. Countries that weren't drawn for the dance panel included the United States, Canada,

Pelletier and Jamie Salé practice at the Delta Center in Salt Lake City.

Above: **Canadian figure skating judge Benoit Lavoie arrives at a news conference in St. Foy, Quebec, on Tuesday February 26, 2002. He denied pressuring others to vote for Salé and Pelletier, who were later awarded Olympic gold in figure skating after winning the silver.**

and France. The absence of France on the dance panel changed everything.

The French skating federation had few cards to play at the Olympic Games. Out of four skating disciplines, they had drawn only one judge on one panel—the pairs event. Le Gougne was the federation's only tool. The only French skaters in line for an Olympic medal of any kind were ice dancers Marina Anissina and Gwendal Peizerat. Anissina and Peizerat were worthy of Olympic gold and, in the real world, they shouldn't have needed political help to win the ice dancing event. But the ice dancing event isn't part of the real world, and hasn't been for years. Results don't always match performances, and in the year leading up to the Olympic Games, it appeared that the agenda had already been set. There was a strong political push behind Italian, Russian, and Israeli dance teams. And a Ukrainian team was doing wonderfully well, too. Talent didn't seem to matter.

In that sort of climate, France made a deal with the devil, sources said, specifying that in return for Le Gougne placing Russians Elena Berezhnaia and Anton Sikharulidze first in the pairs event, the Russian camp and its allies would help Anissina and Peizerat in

French ice skating judge Marie-Reine Le Gougne arrives before the start of the pairs short program competition at the Winter Olympics in Salt Lake City. This time there were no tears or tirades as the French judge embroiled in the figure skating scandal calmly told investigators that she voted for the Russian pairs team on merit and not as part of any scheme to fix the event.

Stephen Stills, of Crosby, Stills, Nash and Young, parades on stage during their concert with a sign supporting Canadian figure skaters Salé and Pelletier in Toronto. Reaction to the judges' decision, a 5–4 split that gave the pairs gold to Russians Elena Berezhnaia and Anton Sikharulidze ahead of Salé and Pelletier, ranged from outrage to more restrained analysis.

International Skating Union president Ottavio Cinquanta speaks at a press conference, following a meeting of the 11-member council of the ISU in Salt Lake City on Monday, February 18, 2002. The meeting was held to discuss a reform package, following the judging controversy in the pairs figure skating competition at the 2002 Winter Olympic Games.

the ice dancing event. "The Russians desperately need first place in pairs with Berezhnaia and Sikharulidze," said sources, without specifying the reason for the desperate need. Russian/Soviet pairs skaters had won the past 10 Olympic gold medals, dating back to 1964, and undoubtedly, it would have been demoralizing for them to lose their dominance. And overall at the Salt Lake City Olympics, the Russians finished only fifth as a nation, with 17 medals, behind Germany, United States, Norway, and Austria, only six of them gold. It was the worst effort by Soviets or Russians since they joined the Olympic fold in 1956. At home later, Leonid Tyagachev, head of the Russian Olympic Committee, faced questions about the national's teams "failures," and finally blamed the problems on a money shortage, as well as unfair treatment by North American officials.

But long before the medal wins-and-losses stories began to be played out, sources say that had Berezhnaia and Sikharulidze lost the gold in the pairs event, there would have been a powerful Russian push to put their ice dancers Irina Lobacheva and Ilia Averbukh on top of the podium in the other skating discipline. As it was, the Russian ice dancers almost won too. They lost a five-four judges' split in the free dance, with five judges voting for the French, four opting for the Russians. The Russians took the silver and afterward Shekhovtseva was heard angrily laying the blame for their loss on the judges who did not support them.

There were other political factors at stake with the French pair judge, too, beyond the Olympic Games. Sources say Le Gougne came under pressure from the Eastern bloc to place the Russian pair first also because she was up for election in June to get onto the International Skating Union's figure-skating technical committee. Since the breakup of the Soviet Union into a scattering of independent countries, and therefore a mass of different skating federations, the Russian/Eastern bloc countries have held a lot of voting cards in Congress elections.

As for Le Gougne, she became the lightning rod of the judging scandal at the Olympic Games. At the routine judges' event review the day after the pairs final, the judges discussed their work with referee Ron Pfenning, the event coordinator, in a room that had been taped shut with duct tape so that nobody could eavesdrop on the proceedings. Le Gougne, at first sitting quietly, suddenly blurted out that she had been pressured by her federation, led by Didier Gailhaguet, and begged for help. This came after Pfenning, an American, had expressed displeasure with the results; on his own scorecard he had placed Salé and Pelletier first, although the referees' marks are not taken into account in the scoring. In this atmosphere, Gailhaguet's name came tumbling from Le Gougne's trembling lips. Pfenning, widely known as a fair official, filed a report to International Skating Union president Ottavio Cinquanta, who interviewed Le Gougne personally. Le Gougne told Cinquanta the same story, and then signed a written statement that she had been pressured by Gailhaguet to vote for the Russians. "What she said and what she signed was something that she reviewed," Cinquanta said. "She looked at it."

Based on a cursory investigation of the outburst and several signed reports, on February 14 Cinquanta and the International Skating Union council voted unanimously to suspend Le Gougne for misconduct, which included failing to notify the referee of coming under pressure to predetermine results. But already, Le Gougne was starting to change her story in public statements to media. Cinquanta appeared taken aback by this news in a press conference announcing her suspension. He had known nothing of her latest remarks.

Signed statement or not, the stories began to change with the suddeness of a Florida rainstorm. First, Gailhaguet denied pressuring Le Gougne. Then Le Gougne denied that Gailhaguet had pressured her. Not everybody bought it. Katsuichiro Hisanaga, a vice-president of the International Skating Union from Japan, said that Gailhaguet had pressured judges in the past and should be kicked out of the union if he had indeed forced a French judge to cheat at the Olympics. Hisanaga said it wasn't the first time Gailhaguet had pressured judges. Gailhaguet countered by saying Hisanaga had never contributed anything of importance to the skating federation and should stifle his comments.

But Le Gougne wasn't stifling her comments. She told L'*Equipe*, the French sports daily, that she had never made any kind of deal at all. "I judged in my soul and conscience," she told the French magazine. "I considered the Russians were the best. I never made a deal with an official or a Russian judge." Hisanaga didn't believe this either, noting that she had already admitted to the pressure, and that it came from Gailhaguet. "Day after day, the story is changed," he said.

New stories came in torrents, mostly from Le Gougne. She also told L'*Equipe* that she felt threatened on the shuttle back to the hotel, where she said Sally Stapleford, chairperson of the figure skating technical committee of the International Skating Union, "assailed me, scolding me for having voted for the Russians. That's when I broke down." And she didn't stop there. Le Gougne also told the French daily that it was Stapleford who came up with the idea

Didier Gailhaguet, head of the French Olympic committee and the country's figure skating federation, speaks at a news conference at the French House in downtown Salt Lake City, Thursday, February 14, 2002. Three days after Salé and Pelletier received gold medals to match the ones the Russians already had, judge Marie-Reine Le Gougne formally recanted her allegation that she was pressured into a vote-swapping deal. Asked why she had named Gailhaguet as the one who had pressured her into voting for the Russians over a Canadian pair, Miller said, "She did it to escape further pressure, to deflect criticism."

Salé and Pelletier compete in the pairs free program in the Winter Olympics.

that Gailhaguet pressured her to vote, and that Stapleford was part of a Canadian conspiracy to reverse the decision.

However, a cluster of reports told a different story. U.S. skating judge Jon Jackson, a lawyer in California who did not work at the Olympics, witnessed Le Gougne's meeting with Stapleford in the hotel lobby and said the French judge had volunteered all of the information. At least four parties witnessed the incident, he said. Her suggestions of Stapleford's actions were "ridiculous, indicating that people were running scared," he added. He told reporters that Le Gougne spouted to Stapleford: "Ice dancing is ruining the sport of figure skating. I have to defend myself. I did this for my dance team. It's a deal with the Russians, first place for first place."

Stapleford, who has been the champion of honest judging since

Russian pair Elena Berezhnaia and Anton Sikharulidze perform during a pairs short program practice.

she took her post years ago, said the French judge ran off in a very emotional state. Born and raised in Britain, Stapleford holds a Canadian passport because her father was a Canadian hockey player. She filed a report to Pfenning of what she had seen and heard, signed by two other respected committee members, Walburga Grimm of Germany and Britta Lindgren of Sweden.

The stakes and furore over the incident were blowing sky high and it was the topic of conversation around the world. Cinquanta, the champion of secrecy, called for an internal investigation, and at first wouldn't reveal how many and just who would be on this special commission. Before long it came out. The commission consisted of two men, Gerhard Zimmerman, the first vice-president for the International Skating Union, representing speedskating, and the union's legal adviser, Gerhardt Bubnik of the Czech Republic. Gailhaguet testified in front of them for 45 minutes in Salt Lake City, denying everything. Le Gougne sat in front of the commission members for three hours with a couple of high-priced Salt Lake City lawyers, Max Miller and Erik Christiansen. There, she recanted her signed statement, denied what others said about her emotional outburst after the pairs event, and also denied any deal and any

Sally Stapleford of Britain, chairperson of the Figure Skating Techinical Committee, grimaces while being questioned by the media as she arrives for a meeting of the 11-member council of the International Skating Union, at a hotel in Salt Lake City, Monday, February 18, 2002, held to discuss a reform package, following the judging controversy in the pairs figure skating competition.

vote-swapping. With the help of her lawyers, Le Gougne stated that she implicated Gailhaguet as the one who pressured her to vote for the Russians as a way to escape further pressure and deflect criticism. In spite of the hot water in which Le Gougne found herself, her goal was to become reinstated as a judge. At the time, the International Skating Union had not defined the length of her suspension; she could face permanent suspension.

Shortly after she testified, Le Gougne spoke again, and with the help of her lawyers, told the *New York Times* that from the time she was named as an Olympic judge, she encountered pressure from Canadian officials to place Salé and Pelletier first, specifying that the lobbying was led by senior Canadian skating officials and one powerful International Skating Union official with ties to Canada, perhaps a reference to Stapleford.

"It was going to be very close," she told the newspaper. "I was in the middle." She added that on the night before the pairs short program, Canadian judge Benoit Lavoie invited her along with 10 other people to a birthday party for a Polish judge on the ice dancing panel and there, they exchanged gifts and made champagne toasts. Le Gougne said she was shocked by all of this, believing that the aim of the Canadians was to secure votes for Canadian ice dancers Shae-Lynn Bourne and Victor Kraatz from the Polish judge in the ice dancing event. On the final day of the Olympics, her revelation took Canadian skating officials by surprise and sent them into their burrows for a day or two of silence.

When the dust settled, Pfenning told reporters that Le Gougne had never mentioned pressure from Canadians before. Michael Chambers, president of the Canadian Olympic Association dismissed the claims. International Olympic Committee member Paul Henderson, a Canadian, thundered, "She has never, ever stood up and said why she scored the way she did. All she's talking about is pressuring. It tells me that she's like what the French said: that she's very nervous and her psyche's very fragile, and this has proven it." After arriving home in Montreal, Lavoie denied Le Gougne's allegations that he tried to sway any votes at the birthday party. He said the party was organized by the Polish federation, which invited 27 judges to a room at the Westcoast Hotel. "Everyone received the same invitation," he said. "We all went there, and I brought a cake. That's the only thing." Lavoie insisted that Canada was not involved in any vote-swapping scheme. He confirmed that 12 people in the event review meeting heard Le Gougne blame French Olympic chef de mission Gailhaguet for pressuring her to award the gold medal to the Russian skaters rather than Salé and Pelletier. There was no mistake that

Lavoie had heard her: he had sat next to Le Gougne at the meeting. "All I can say is that I've never had trouble sleeping," the Canadian judge said, adding that he did have trouble understanding the enormous pressure that supposedly rested on Le Gougne's shoulders. "We're trained for it," he said. "We all have pressure. [Le Gougne] had experience. She's been to the Olympics before."

One theme seems clear: everyone had stopped talking about the involvement of the Russians or anyone else in all of the deals. Or that the assistant referee of the pairs event was a Russian, Alexander Lakernik. If the French had indeed been making deals with somebody, who were they making them with? Cinquanta stated in a news conference that he had no evidence of any kind of collusion among judges from different disciplines, but then, he was the man who told skaters, coaches, and officials at the closing banquet for the 2001 world championships in Vancouver that the results of the ice dancing event in that competition were correct, and that everybody should just accept them. These comments came after a team from his country had won, sparking a firestorm of protest among spectators, coaches, and other skaters who felt that Barbara Fusar-Poli and Maurizio Margaglio were not as talented as some of the couples ranked below them.

The makeup of the judging panel there, too, was suspect. At that event, Ukrainian judge Yuri Balkov had shown up on the ice dancing panel, although he had not been originally accreditated to represent his country. Although he was the judge who was suspended for a year for rhyming off the results of the 1998 Olympic ice dancing event to Canadian judge Jean Senft over the telephone before the event was over, Balkov somehow received accreditation, contravening International Skating Union rules, which don't brook this kind of substitution. Balkov was back judging on the ice dancing panel at the Salt Lake City Olympics, too.

With the judging irregularities of the pairs event already on the world's front pages, one would have thought that the ice dancing judges in Salt Lake City would have been diving for cover, judging their event the way it was supposed to be judged to save their skins. Before the pairs scandal, there had already been calls from IOC member Richard Pound to drop ice dancing from the Olympics because of dodgy judging in the past. However, on the morning of the free dance, sources say Russians were still busy lobbying for top placements for Lobacheva and Averbukh.

After the scandal in the pair skating event, Lithuanian ice dancers Margarita Drobiazko and Povilas Vanagas were some who hoped that the judging in ice dancing would improve. They found that it did not. After judges placed them fifth, the Lithuanian skating federation and its tiny Olympic committee protested the results of the ice dancing event, saying that judges had not made the proper deductions for mistakes or illegal moves made by three couples ahead of them, including Russian, Italian, and Canadian teams. The 1984 Olympic champion Jayne Torvill, who was commentating for the British Broadcasting Corporation, backed them, saying on air she thought the Lithuanians should have finished second in the free dance. The Lithuanians staged a news conference at the Olympics, at first saying they did not want to comment on the judging but, after years of frustrations and now sitting in front of a large room full people who wanted to listen, they spilled amazing details about the judging world.

Most significantly, they said Russia and the former Soviet states are at the root of the judging problems. "Usually what takes place when former Soviet Union judges are on the panel, many, many more games are played," Vanagas said. "They were really the ones in the last 10 years who were making the most of the dangerous dirty game situations in ice dancing." The Lithuanians said the Grand Prix Final in Kitchener, Ontario, in December 2001 was like a breath of fresh air to them, because, for once, there was no Russian judge on the panel, and for once the majority of judges voted according to what they saw on the ice. In that event, five of the seven judges—from France, Germany, Canada, United States, and Lithuania—created a major breakthrough for their discipline. The crowd was excited; for a change, they didn't know who was going to win.

Others weren't so thrilled with this turn of events in Kitchener. Behind the scenes, the Russian-Italian influence was at work. When Fusar-Poli and Margaglio were dumped to fourth, while skating the routine that won them their world title, an unhappy Cinquanta was seen drawing referee Alexander Gorshkov into a room for a chat before the judges' event review meeting. During the meeting, Gorshkov then astonished the honest judges when he scolded them for their efforts, told them they had set ice dancing back 15 years and asked them to write multiple letters of explanation for many of their placements. His actions smacked of intimidation. The Russian substitute judge—whose scores did not count—placed the Italians first. Gorshkov's placements tallied up in such a way that he had placed the Italians first, as well. Gorshkov was also the referee Cinquanta chose for the Olympic Games.

The Russians had also been at work at the scandal-plagued Nagano Olympics, when the judging of ice dancing was dragged onto the carpet, and afterward, *L'Equipe*, a daily sports magazine based in France, quoted Russian federation president Valentin Piseev's advice to Russian judges: "Vote the way I tell you or stay at home." None of this surprised Drobiazko and Vanagas, who actually won the bronze medal ahead of the Italians in Kitchener. The lobbying by strong federations, such as the Russian ones, means there are strong connections between the results of one discipline and another, Vanagas said. Drobiazko said they already knew when they arrived at the Olympic Games that they would be battling for fourth and fifth place with the Canadian dance team of Bourne and Kraatz. "Even though they [Bourne and Kraatz] won the Grand Prix Final, they had no judge," Drobiazko said. Had there been a Canadian judge on the Olympic ice dancing panel, Bourne and Kraatz would likely have been fighting for second place, Vanagas said. "That's a sad story." he said. The Canadians finished fourth.

Not all of the judges are dishonest, Vanagas continued. "Some of the judges are really trying to be independent. That's great that such judges exist." The honest judges tend to come from the United States, whose federation doesn't seem to play the deal-making games very well; Britain; Switzerland; Japan; Australia; and others, Drobiazko and Vanagas said. American skaters Elizabeth Punsalan and Jerod Swallow suffered badly at the Nagano Olympics, finishing only seventh behind the hapless Italians, something that bothers the Lithuanians to this day. Drobiazko and Vanagas were eighth in that event.

However, the other disciplines are not at all immune from what happens in the ice dancing events, and none of the skaters seemed surprised. Drobiazko and Vanagas hope only that judges in the future will be sincere, honest, and not too dependent on their federations.

The Lithuanians themselves have no strong federation to back them. They are from a country of only 3.5 million with a small group of people forming their federation, and as Vanagas says, "We feel very much that we are dumped down." Before the Olympic Games, they had never complained or filed a protest before, mostly because they didn't know that they could. "I was not afraid to say what I thought, but I was afraid nobody would listen to me," Drobiazko said. "But the Olympic Games are a different story. It is time to say now." With only the world championships left in their careers, Drobiazko and Vanagas have little now to lose. They say they spoke out in Salt Lake City mostly to help young skaters in the future. Salé and Pelletier promise to make it their cause, too. The Olympics began to air the dirty laundry, and now the International Skating Union has a lot of cleaning to do.

Happy Ending

Growing up in small Canadian towns couldn't possibly have prepared Jamie Salé and David Pelletier for the firestorm of outrage that flamed around the world for the first week of the Olympic Games in Salt Lake City. The two Canadians responded the only way they knew how: with decency. Pelletier admitted he felt guilty that he had stolen attention away from athletes in other sports. They didn't blame the Russian pairs, Elena Berezhnaia and Anton Sikharulidze, who defeated them. They put on smiling faces, and celebrated with the Barenaked Ladies, a Canadian band. They tried their best to have fun. But they were quickly finding out that their lives were no longer their own.

Salé and Pelletier had scarcely a moment to breathe during the judging controversies that raged over their heads for at least a week. The outrage was worldwide and quickly involved Canadian Prime Minister Jean Chrétien, U.S. President George Bush, who found time to throw his support behind the Canadian pair, and Russian president Vladimir Putin, standing firm behind the Russian pair. The young Canadian pair wasn't immune to the intense media interest. For the 48 hours after they won the silver medal, they had little sleep. After the pairs long program, they finally fell asleep at 7:30 a.m., arose three hours later, and did 13 straight hours of interviews. *Larry King Live* wanted them. Jay Leno wanted them, offering a chartered jet to fly them from Salt Lake City to Burbank, California, and back. During the first week, their agent, Craig Fenech, said he fielded 150 to 200 media requests a day. "I'm starting to get tired of listening to myself," Pelletier said wearily.

The aftermath of the scandal overwhelmed the small-town athletes completely. Half-awake, Pelletier could charm audiences and talk-show hosts with his witty lines. Still, he admitted he also felt like a target, even a criminal, for having to explain whether or not they had a good relationship with Berezhnaia and Sikharulidze, and whether they had spoken with them. "We didn't come to this Olympics to have this happen to us," Salé said. "We are tired. We are exhausted. We are constantly having people come up to us and want to talk to us." However, their silver medal had become worth

Salé is thrown by her partner during their short program in the pairs competition.

much more than the gold. Pelletier's mother, Murielle, said it best: she told them their silver medals were like platinum. "That's the best, right?" Salé asked.

It got better. The scandal immediately spurred a gathering of Canadian political resources to lobby both the International Skating Union and the International Olympic Committee to resolve the issues quickly, in case Cinquanta might drag out an investigation until after the Olympic Games had finished and interest in the subject had died down. Canadian International Olympic Committee member Richard Pound, who had publicly spoken out about irregularities in ice dancing, now had a bigger issue, and he continued to apply pressure to IOC president Jacques Rogge, pointing out that the scandals were ruining the Olympic franchise. American Olympic officials also quietly pitched in with legal help, concerned that they, too, had been victims of deal-making among international judging. U.S. pair skaters Kyoko Ina and John Zimmerman had skated the

In Moscow, Prime Minister Jean Chretien and his wife Aline congratulate Salé and Pelletier after it was announced that they were awarded the Gold Medal by the International Olympic Committee.

Far Left: **Salé is lifted by her partner during the exhibition at the Olympic Winter Games.**

72

A Figure Skating Gala: Pelletier is thrown by Salé during the exhibition at the Winter Olympics.

Salé and Pelletier fall in the closing seconds of their pairs short program.

Far Right: Co-Gold medalists Jamie Salé and Elena Berezhnaia share a hug as Anton Sikharulidze and David Pelletier look on after being presented thier gold medals. A happy ending to an on-going controversy.

Salé and Pelletier carry the Canadian flag during the closing ceremonies for the 2002 Olympic Games.

best performances of the night, stirring the crowd to a thunderous ovation, and were placed only fifth.

In the end, the International Olympic Committee awarded a second set of gold medals to Salé and Pelletier, after the International Skating Union, under pressure to come to a swift resolution, agreed to render void the work of Marie-Reine Le Gougne. This move placed Salé and Pelletier in a tie with Elena Berezhnaia and Anton Sikharulidze, and hence, the decision to give a second set of medals. Salé and Pelletier were thrilled by the decision. It was only the fourth time in Olympic history that a second set of gold medals had been awarded. Some observers believed that, either way, Salé and Pelletier couldn't lose. The more people talked about what happened to them, the higher their visibility.

Sikharulidze figured it out very quickly. After arriving home in Moscow, Sikharulidze said: "If everything were to go quietly, nobody would watch the games, there would not be enough interest with the general public. It is cool the way it is." With a cool head, he said the decision to give Salé and Pelletier a second gold medal didn't show an anti-Russian bias at all. "Even if six more gold medals were awarded, it would not have decreased the value of my victory," said Sikharulidze, who admitted he lost five pounds over the scandal.

The awarding of the second gold medal may not have increased the value of Salé and Pelletier's appeal, either. They already had it, in spades. Before they even left the Olympic Games, they inked a lucrative endorsement deal with Proctor & Gamble, to promote Crest Whitestrips, a new toothpaste product. Is anybody smiling more broadly than Salé and Pelletier? In all, Salé and Pelletier could be expected to earn up to $US5 million ($C8 million) a year from product endorsements and appearances if they opted to turn professional on the spot. The figures are far higher than what most other Canadian athletes make. With their attractive appearance, their personality, and integrity, Salé and Pelletier have been a marketer's dream. Salé and Pelletier, the small-town kids, suddenly developed international appeal.

But the story isn't over. The second gold medal solved no long-standing judging problems. After they were awarded second gold medals, the Canadian Olympic Association dropped its call for an independent investigation. The International Skating Union proposed an overhaul of the marking and judging system that would, in effect, make it impossible to know how any judge voted. It also proposed an overhaul of ice dancing rules after the Nagano Olympics, but it soon became clear that the new rules didn't stop the political games, because some judges just ignored the rules

anyway. International Skating Union elections are coming up in June, and nobody wants to lose the Russian/Eastern bloc vote, including perhaps, Cinquanta. Salvation is a long way off.

But salvation has to start somewhere. At the Salt Lake City Olympics, it started with two young people with big ideas from small Canadian towns. They took one step at a time. They did everything right. They dreamed the right dreams. They conquered their demons. And when nobody was looking, they presented Berezhnaia and Sikharulidze with two little gifts, wrapped in gold. Two crystal hearts were inside. Yes, Salé and Pelletier made all the difference.

Salé and Pelletier on ice during their controversial pairs free skating performance.

Only time will tell to what heights Salé and Pelletier will rise in the world of figure skating.